Your Resiliency GPS

A Guide for Growing through Life and Work

EILEEN McDARGH

Your Resiliency GPS: A Guide for Growing through Life and Work

ISBN-10: 0-9623190-5-8
ISBN-13: 978-0-9623190-5-1

Self-publishing Partners: Studio 6 Sense, LLC • studio6sense.com

*To my sweet William, who makes it possible
for me to breathe in this world*

*To my sister Susan and my twin brother John,
support crew since the very beginning*

PRAISE FOR
Your Resiliency GPS

Anyone who knows Eileen McDargh knows she is a ray of sunshine in an often cloudy world. As important, her work and ideas have substance and create powerful results. *Your Resiliency GPS* will provide you with new ideas and tools that we all need to face the challenges of life.

Mark Sanborn, Author, The Fred Factor

I really loved this book. It is chock full of powerful tools, questions, and suggestions on how to grow through just about anything that life throws at you. The Resiliency GPS is brilliant. Who doesn't need a GPS to navigate life's challenges more easily? You'll never feel lost. The best part is that you arrive at your "destination" in a better place than you had imagined. Thank you so much for guiding us Eileen.

Lorna Riley, CEO, Chart Learning Solutions
www.chartlearningsolutions

Every life has tough moments, and Eileen McDargh is a master at helping people deal with those moments. Her book, *Your Resiliency GPS*, which contains some of her best ideas on moving through adversity, is an inspiring treasure.

Mark Levy, Author, Accidental Genius: Using Writing
to Generate Your Best Ideas, Insight, and Content

According to Oliver Wendell Holmes, Jr. "A mind that is stretched by a new experience can never go back to its old dimensions." There is no bouncing back to normal. This is the central theme of *Your Resiliency GPS*. Eileen McDargh challenges you to embrace the challenges of life and then gives you the GPS (Growth Potential Strategy) to guide you on the journey. Buy this book and start today.

Stan Phelps, Founder of 9 INCH marketing,
Forbes contributor and Author of *Purple Goldfish,*
Green Goldfish, and *Golden Goldfish*

As surely as Robert Cialdini showed us exactly how to influence others, Eileen McDargh wisely describes how to turn challenging times into opportunities to become more alive and resilient.

Kare Anderson, Author, *Mutuality Matters*

I randomly opened the book at a number of pages. Each time, I smiled and felt both lighter and stronger at the same time. The quotes, stories and easy to implement action steps in *Your Resiliency GPS* actually rewired my brain to embrace change. This book isn't momentary motivation; the pages provide long-lasting hope and joy.

Marcia Reynolds, PsyD, Author of *The Discomfort Zone:*
How Leaders Turn Difficult Conversations into
Breakthroughs and *Outsmart Your Brain*

I love this book! It's crammed with solid advice, hard-won wisdom, and powerful probing questions! Eileen doesn't stop with just this book. She continues your learning through a constantly updated resource page on her web site!

Jesse Stoner, Author, *Full Steam Ahead*

Sooner or later you'll cotton on to the fact that if you're not enjoying the journey, what's the point of the end destination? This is a practical book that will help you maintain your focus, grow your courage and develop your resilience, so that your journey inspires you and nourishes you.

Michael Bungay Stanier
Senior Partner, Box of Crayons

No one quite approaches the subject like Eileen. She draws on a life of experience, lived fully, and thought about deeply. She knows a lot and she shares a lot.

Sprinkled throughout are some amazing insightful "realculating questions" that Eileen poses to her readers. These questions themselves are worth the price of the book. Actually if you take time to answer just 1/4 of them, you'll quadruple your investment!

Bev Kaye, Founder Career Systems International,
Author of *Love it. Don't Leave it*. And many more!

There's something very special about *Your Resiliency GPS*. It's more than a book, it's a life-enhancing GPS system to carry with you as you traverse through the ups and downs. Eileen McDargh does a masterful job of mixing topical research, practical advice, and colorful–and often profound–stories. I just bought ten copies ... you should too!

Bill Treasurer, Author, *Leaders Open Doors*
and *Courage Goes to Work*.

"This book offers a clear path to core skills that everyone needs. Listen to Eileen's wise advice. You can't get much out of life if you don't learn how to be resilient!

Kathy B. Dempsey, Author, *Shed or You're Dead*

CONTENTS

FOREWORD

I first met Eileen on a day she'd received a standing ovation at a large healthcare conference. Her slides had gone haywire right in the middle of her presentation, a crisis that would have thrown many speakers for a loop. But Eileen – the Queen of Resiliency – turned that apparent disaster into an opportunity to connect more closely with her audience. This is the book I have been waiting for ever since that day. *Your Resiliency GPS* is a practical roadmap for practicing what Eileen calls "presilience" (preemptive resilience). It's jam-packed with **(GPS)** Growth Potential Strategies, Recalculating Questions, and Resiliency Skills to help you overcome and grow through the inevitable challenges, obstacles, and setbacks in your life.

You have no doubt heard the saying that when one door closes another one opens. You might even believe it, at least in a theoretical sense. But for you to take advantage of that newly opened door, two things must happen. First, you must actually see the other door open. Second, you must have the gumption to walk through it.

In this book Eileen will challenge you to broaden your perspective to see opportunities where others might see only barriers – to see open doors where others see only brick walls. She will share practical ideas for developing the character strength and fortitude that you must have to use adversity and opportunity as the springboard for personal growth and achievement.

Every great accomplishment was once the "impossible" dream of a dreamer who refused to quit regardless of the obstacles and setbacks. *Your Resiliency GPS* will help you transform your "impossible" dreams of today into your reality of tomorrow. *Reading and absorbing these lessons will be one of the best investments you ever make in yourself and in your dreams.*

Joe Tye, CEO and Head Coach of Values Coach Inc.

Author, *All Hands on Deck: 8 Essential Lessons for Building a Culture of Ownership*

ACKNOWLEDGEMENTS

Lorna Riley, you literally gave me three full days of your precious time to read every word, question order, apply punctuation, monitor spacing and be THE EDITOR of my dreams—all because you are my friend!!! How can I ever thank you?

Dear sweet Jesse Stoner—my sounding board, my wordsmith, my dear dear practical guide who said "Just get it out". You teach me so much. You rock. Thank you.

Joe Tye, without your ideas and recommendation, I would never have found Lisa Peterson. You have offered advice and insight that helped solidify concepts on the book. You believe in me. I am so grateful.

Bonnie Jo Davis, for all you do and for how much you care, thank you so much!

Introduction

～～～～～～～

WE'RE ALL ON THE SAME ROAD

Surprises are the new normal. Change is the new constant. The past doesn't look like the present. Whether you are…

> » leading a Fortune 100 company, a small department, or an enterprise of one…

> » trying to reinvent your career, launch a new product, or juggle the demands of aging parents and children…

> » leaving the confines of an unhappy marriage to launch your small self into a brand new strange place…

> » struggling with the loss of anything from a job to a loved one…

> » wanting your employees to be excited by change rather than terrified…

…wherever you find yourself in this moment, the ability to cultivate and practice resiliency is critical.

Resilience is a way of walking though life.

It is about our personal energy to keep on keeping on. It means discovering what drains our energy and what renews it. It means developing stamina and staying power.

And this book will show you how.

Are you ready???

Time to turn it around… to discover internal resources for reclaiming, renewing, and restoring the energy that sparks your resilient spirit. That's what this book is all about: giving you ideas, tools, links, and systems to revive and renew the spark of hope, optimism and self-leadership.

I write this book for myself as much as for you. We teach what we most need to learn. I am aware that this is an emotional journey, an intellectual exercise, and a spiritual roadway. It will take heart, head, and hands.

Is this a self-development book? Yes. Everything starts with the self.

Is this a leadership book? Yes. All leadership starts with self-leadership.

It is my hope that you discover an energy source that requires no wells, no fracking, no deep drilling, or nuclear rods. Your SOULar power is renewable and sustainable. May you be rewarded with strength beyond measure and the ability to transform the life of your work and the work of your life.

Dump
The
Dictionary!

As I explored the wisdom we all get in hindsight, I realized that there is another word we might use: **PREsilience** (preemptive resilience). *These are skills and actions that can be cultivated, developed, and taken BEFORE necessity strikes. It is about being pro-active and prepared.* If not prepared and proactive, your head will resonate with after-the-fact "if onlys."

In short, human resiliency is far deeper and more all encompassing than how the dictionary defines "resilience."

Definition of *RESILIENCE* from Merriam Webster:

1. The capability of a strained body to recover its size and shape after deformation caused especially by compressive stress.

2. An ability to recover from or adjust easily to misfortune or change.

Inherent in the first definition is the notion of returning to an original size and shape. This might be true for bent metal, but it is not enough for people in this global 24/7 world. In fact, the common phase, "bounce back" works for tennis balls, blow-up clowns, and trampolines but not for the human system. Instead, true resilience is the ability to *grow forward through challenge or opportunity, becoming wiser, smarter, stronger, and better able to create a sustainable future.*

There is NO bouncing back! No! Not! Never! Going <u>back</u> to an original state might feel comfortable but it denies the very opportunity of personal and organizational growth. In a constantly changing world, returning to old habits, old structures, and old behaviors can actually be counter-productive. Growing forward contains more power.

Today, resiliency also means one is willing to turn right when everyone else turns left. It implies courage, tenacity, and taking the uncharted course. For an individual, it also means listening deeply to one's inner voice rather than the chorus that surrounds you.

The second dictionary definition is hampered by the words "adjust easily," "misfortunc," and "changc." Lct's examine those words.

Resilience is seriously hard work, requiring body, mind, and spirit to be engaged. It requires learning from errors and that takes humility. It can take collaboration and connecting with others and that takes interpersonal skills. Some parts might be easier than others, but all adjustment requires effort.

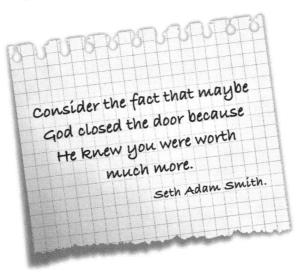

Consider the fact that maybe God closed the door because He knew you were worth much more.

Seth Adam Smith.

"Misfortune" is a word that belittles the tremendous turn of events many of our brothers and sisters face on a daily basis. My friend W. Mitchell—an amazing keynote speaker—leaves audiences spellbound with his story of losing his fingers, his face, and suffering 3rd and 4th degree burns over most of his body, only to become a paraplegic four years later in a plane crash. One would never call these accidents "misfortunes." Call them horrible. Terrifying. Life-threatening. And ultimately, Mitchell took these events and shaped his life in ways to make him more powerful than ever before.

Likewise, great opportunities rather than "misfortunes" might demand our energy, strength, determination, and courage. It takes resilience to find the resources to build an incredible cardiac hospital network like Narayana Hrudayalaya in India (a 98% success rate in cardiac surgeries), or to seize the worldwide need for potable water and create—as Matt Damon did www.water.org.

Lastly, there's Webster's phrase "recover from... change." Such a catchall statement! There are many kinds of changes and some don't require "recovery" but rather rejoicing. Think of the birth of a child, a long-awaited promotion, a move into retirement, a wedding day, and perhaps the momentous day graduates throw up their mortar board and declare themselves free of college (even if burdened with debt).

Resilience is about sustaining an organization, a life, a relationship. Resilience is complex, multidimensional,

We always experience anxiety when faced with opportunity.

Sam Horn

personal as well as professional. It's about growing through the dark night of the soul and finding sunrise on the other side. **Presilience** is practicing it now, building pre-emptive resources within yourself, your organization, your world.

WHAT YOU WILL DISCOVER

In this book you will find your resiliency **GPS**, *Growth Potential Strategy,* to help wherever you are on the resiliency road. The **GPS** will be identified by this icon. It will guide you towards a more desirable destination.

As you read the action strategies, you will also see **Recalculating Questions** to put the strategies into play. You may choose how to use these questions. However, *I strongly recommend* that you get a blank book—maybe even one of those old-fashioned black/ white mottled composition books. Here is why: writing clears our minds and lets us return time and again to our thoughts. The Recalculating Questions might also provide grist for a conversation with a trusted friend. If you only read the book and do nothing, nothing will change.

The overarching benefit of thinking, writing, and doing is that you will become stronger over time.

Nature Or Nurture?

THE SURPRISING ANSWER

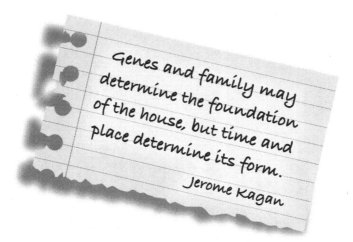

Genes and family may determine the foundation of the house, but time and place determine its form.

Jerome Kagan

am an observer and researcher of human behavior and interaction.

I marvel at the amazing things individuals can do against great odds and groan when confronted with rigid beliefs and actions that defeat any chance for resiliency and sustainability. And I groan even deeper when the rigidity is my own.

I've read the documents by researchers who are trying to determine if resiliency is partially genetic and partially a response to the environment. While there continues to be genetic research, as well as concern over children who grow up in high-risk environments, the reality is that a majority of us are hard-wired to be resilient.

In her article, *The Foundations Of Resiliency Framework,* Bonnie Bernard M.S.W. writes:

We are all born with innate resiliency, with the capacity to develop the traits commonly found in resilient survivors: social competence (responsiveness, cultural flexibility, empathy, caring, communication skills, and a sense of humor); problem-solving (planning, help-seeking, critical and creative thinking); autonomy (sense of identity, self-efficacy, self-awareness, task-mastery, and adaptive distancing from negative messages and conditions); and a sense of purpose and belief in a bright future (goal direction, educational aspirations, optimism, faith, and spiritual connectedness). Benard, 1991.

In Bernard's work, she concludes that we have an inborn capacity for transformation and change.

Fast forward to 2012. Dr. Steven Southwick and Dr. Dennis Charney amass 20 years of research for their book *Resilience: The Science of Mastering Life's Greatest Challenges*. When their study began, they assumed that resilient people would be rare and somehow genetically gifted. Instead, they discovered that resilience is common and can be seen everywhere. More importantly, they learned that *many people can be trained to become more resilient.*

The good news is that emerging scientific research has shown that neurobiological systems are highly adaptive. Through the brain's neuroplasticity, this mass of gray matter, neurons, and dendrites can rewire itself with practice, persistence, and cognitive training. You can create NEW patterns of thinking and acting that promote resiliency. **Presilience** means you cultivate these new patterns NOW.

In short, the inborn capacity noted in Bernard's work can be strengthened and developed. You can nurture that capacity over time by using the suggestions and action strategies in this book.

Lastly, in the addendum of the book you will find a small assessment of your Resiliency Quotient (RQ). There is one for an individual and one for an organization. You can take it now before reading the book or wait until the end. Either way, it will help you see what are your strengths and what are your opportunities for growth.

Lost is a Place

The journey begins when the luggage is lost.

Anon

J ust as earthquakes are measured on the continuum of a Richter scale, events in our lives fall along the same line. Some are more severe than others. It varies from person to person. What one person might dismiss with the wave of a hand, someone else might struggle to just get up in the morning.

There is no right/wrong, no timetable, and no comparison.

What is required is courage...courage to admit to being lost. Without that courage, your GPS can't kick in.

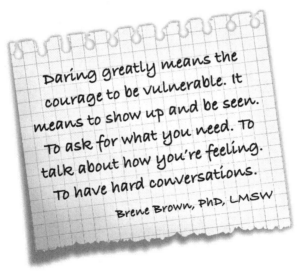

Daring greatly means the courage to be vulnerable. It means to show up and be seen. To ask for what you need. To talk about how you're feeling. To have hard conversations.

Brene Brown, PhD, LMSW

ONE OF MY "LOST" PLACES

It was a combination of things, a swirl of events, emotions, and experiences that left me in a dark spiral of confusion, irrelevance, and depression.

For six years, after moving my Mom to my house and then an assisted living /memory care center two miles away, she had been my primary focus.

I literally would run to her for exercise. I'd be up there every day, sometimes multiple times. I never went out of town unless I knew my sister would be able to drive down from Los Angeles. With Susan and me, Mom had constant love and as many outings as possible until a stroke paralyzed her entire left side.

I would tuck her in bed, sing her goodnight, and bring in Kentucky Fried Chicken to tempt her. My cell phone was my constant companion. After all, with 11 visits to the ER and four hospitalizations, it was my lifeline.

She died in the month of January and the rest of that year was spent handling affairs, arranging a funeral in her home town, sorting out memories, boxes, and items from almost 96 years of living.

Being busy was my "work," aided by three intense international assignments (India, Columbia, Switzerland) that kept me from contemplating what

I wanted in my life now that one door had closed and another might be opening.

I started with looking at my work schedule for the New Year and became horrified by little work, few incoming calls, and no one returning mine. Doing our household budget didn't help matters.

No wonder I woke up with heart palpitations, dreaming that Leonard DiCaprio, the Wolf of Wall Street, was beating me with a ledger sheet and shouting, *"You can't do this!"*

The creep.

But it wasn't just finances.

There was age. When I looked at my life, more years stretched behind me instead of ahead. What was my ACT III and how do I find it? It was a feeling that I no longer brought value to the world and didn't know my place in it.

In short order came a dinner with friends Doug and Carol Baker. Doug had retired as senior vice president for human resources of American Express Financial Advisors. I had just finished reading the book, *True North Groups* that Doug had written with Bill George, now a professor at Harvard Business School and former chair and CEO of Medtronic.

The book spoke about creating personal groups of no more than six people who met at least bi-weekly and supported each other in exploring life questions. Alarmed, I realized, I could not put together six people! My work had carried me across the U.S. and the world, but I had created no local network in my own backyard. Alone. I felt so alone.

The culmination came on the second anniversary of my Mom's death. Because I had intensely cared for her for the last six years of her life, she had become my meaning and focus. Perhaps also my excuse.

That January 28 I could not stop crying. The tears flowed on and off for weeks.

Lost. Scared. Until my ever-wise sister, Susan, explained what was happening.

It's what I went through for nine agonizing months after my precious husband Noam died. It an AFGO: Another F%$^&'& Growth Opportunity.

I had to laugh. Long. Loud.

Susan then gently reminded me of words that numerous psychologists have used: *Remember, this is the fertile void…the threshold to something new. You must hold the space and listen.*

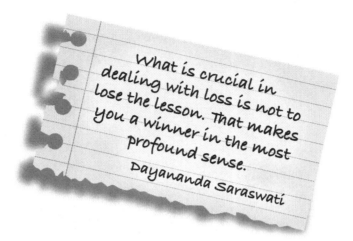

What is crucial in dealing with loss is not to lose the lesson. That makes you a winner in the most profound sense.

Dayananda Saraswati

A WORD ABOUT EMOTIONS

Growing through *opportunity or challenge always brings loss. Even if the move is self-selected and wanted,* there is always loss. What we accepted as our work, our loves, our life, will shift. There is no going back. You can't step into the same river twice. What water caressed your foot yesterday has moved downstream or been evaporated into the clouds overhead.

Grief over loss has no timetable or automatic end. And gender might also make a difference.

Women form their core sense of who they are around their relationships and their relationships are enormously impor-tant to their sense of well-being of who they are in the world. So when women lose a job, they lose something different than men—they lose a connection. They experience mourning.

So states clinical psychologist Judith V. Jordan, director of the Jean Baker Miller Training Institute at

Wellesley Centers for Women and an assistant professor at Harvard Medical School.

On the flip side of the gender coin, men often over-identify with their jobs. How well I remember the editor of a local newspaper who was devastated when his paper merged with a larger regional one and he lost his job.

Who am I now? he moaned. *Before, I could pick up the phone and had access to anyone. Now I am a nobody.* Here started a serious existential crisis and one that was deeply challenging to his spirit.

> Grief is in two parts. The first is loss. The second is the remaking of life.
>
> Anne Roiphe

GPS ACTION

1. Honestly assess your personal situation—essential and difficult to do.

2. Find someone with an open heart to listen—not solve.

3. Practice patience with the unknown.

Setting Your GPS

*If we are facing in the
right direction, all we have to do
is keep on walking.*

Buddha

You're ready to go. Now what? Let's set your GPS by defining your destination.

» Where are you starting from?

» Where do you want to go?

» What do you want to have happen?

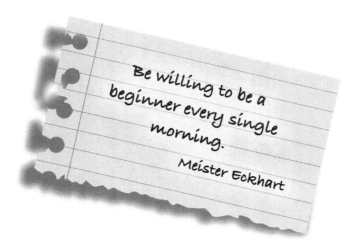

Be willing to be a beginner every single morning.

Meister Eckhart

WHERE ARE YOU STARTING FROM?

Every GPS asks for your current location. You can't start a journey towards resiliency if you can't define where you are right now. You'll read over and over again a request to define your current location. You have to be able to state that clearly in order to know how to move forward.

Your current location might be a place of confusion and anger over a pending merger in your organization. It might be a concern about the health and wellbeing of your family. It might be anxiety over the chance of a lifetime to start your own company or to take a new position. It might be many things.

WHERE DO YOU WANT TO GO?

Your destination can be long-range or short-range. Depending upon the nature of your circumstance, some destinations might be as vague as a foggy horizon. You are not clear exactly where you want to end up. You just know that NOW is not comfortable. In that case, think of incremental destinations—rather like temporary campsites on a hiking trip.

WHAT DO YOU WANT TO HAVE HAPPEN?

In many cases, you seek relief. It can be physical, emotional, or mental. You might want to have innovative ideas generated, new alliances formed, new networks created. You might want clarity and answers.

Additionally, paradox permeates the road to resiliency. On one hand, there are those of us (myself included) who want to just jump in and "fix it." The fix often looks like doing more of the same. In my "lost" example, I wanted answers and nothing came.

There are those who just hope that over time, the situation will resolve itself. No harm. No foul.

The truth rests somewhere in between—unless of course, it's an immediate crisis. Disasters, accidents, and critical events all require fast response.

What will make you more powerful is if you have practiced and planned for those events beforehand.

Example: Emory University Hospital prepared for 12 years to operate a containment unit for patients with dangerous infectious diseases. The unit was built more than a decade ago with consultation from the federal Centers for Disease Control and Prevention. As of this writing, the hospital just admitted two patients with the deadly Ebola virus.

Emory University Hospital had a long-term destination in mind: a containment unit. They practiced what could happen when patients arrived and what medical personnel would need.

In my case, I realized I had not practiced a "what if" scenario. I did not have a destination in mind. I had let my circle of support shrink. I had put all my eggs in one basket without a backup plan.

GPS ACTION

1. You decide if you want to explore a professional challenge/opportunity or a personal challenge/opportunity.

2. In your presilience logbook, write your responses to the recalculating questions. Find someone with whom to have a conversation.

RECALCULATING QUESTIONS

1. What does your situation look like? Define it for your professional or personal situation.

2. What adjectives best describe where you find yourself?

3. What strengths do you have? If you can't think of any, ask someone who knows you well.

4. What people, besides you, are in a similar situation? Do any of them have an interest in growing? Have you asked them?

5. What short-term results do you seek?

6. What long-term results do you seek?

7. How would you recognize forward movement?

For now, all you want is to get a sense of the NOW in your professional or personal world.

Fueling
Your Tank

Energy and persistence conquer all things.
Benjamin Franklin

The current that flows through all of these skills is human energy—the personal equivalent to gasoline.

Energy is the result of meaningful connections that add the spark of potential and possibility—the catalyst for forward momentum.

Think of this like a DNA molecule in which energy weaves through all parts of our life, and if boosted, generates more energy.

Energy is derived from our mental, emotional, and physical hardiness. Consider this the power that drives the human locomotive. Without it, there is no resiliency. In 2008, Psychologists Salvatore Maddi and Suzanne Kobasa coined the term "psychological hardiness." Their research said that individuals could improve their physical and emotional health if they practiced three dimensions:

» Commitment: finding purpose in what you do.

» Control: focusing on what is within your control instead of trying to change something outside of your control.

» Challenge: believing that you can handle whatever comes your way and even if mistakes are inevitable, there is a reason and learning to be had. This means you are change-receptive versus change-adverse. I believe this third C is probably the most difficult to change.

Which leaves you, the reader, with one three-word question:

"Yeah, but how?"

At its most basic definition, energy is the capacity to do work. In order to develop a resilient spirit, we need to identify actions that drain our energy and those which maintain or boost our energy.

GPS ACTION

1. Identify energy-drainers.

2. In your presilience logbook keep track of those events (workload?), people (negativists?), and beliefs (uncertainty?) that just suck the air out of you.

3. Ask for help at work or home with an energy-drainer. Be specific with your request—for example, help with setting boundaries of time and space, delegation, advice, or suggestions. Maybe even asking someone to being available to listen.

4. Identify energy-maintainers.

5. What gives you a lift in your step and a sparkle in your eye? From comfort food to gardening, from playing with children to a long walk with a lover, from breaking bread with friends to having your haircut—you KNOW what renews your energy.

6. Sometimes, handling our energy-drainer creates an energy boost. Example: trying to find files in my office was becoming overwhelming. My office felt like files and papers were ready to dump on my head. With my ever-handy assistant, Bonnie, we went through file drawers and discarded and shredded HUGE bags of paper. The process of cleaning out actually boosted my energy. A draining event turned into an energy boost. Some times it IS the small actions that make a big difference.

7. In your presilience logbook, write your responses to the recalculating questions. Find someone with whom to have a conversation.

RECALCULATING QUESTIONS

1. If you can't change "the event," identify how you can choose to respond to it. Can you amend it? Can you avoid it? Or perhaps you have to accept it?

2. Who has been in this situation before and how can you ask for help?

3. Who can mentor you in the best way?

4. Have you listened to your inner voice?

5. How would a person whom you admire most (living or dead) handle this?

6. What steps does your inner voice of wisdom say you must take?

7. How many items can you list that give you energy?

8. When was the last time you did any of these?

9. What do they cost? Chances are that most activities that give us energy have little to no cost.

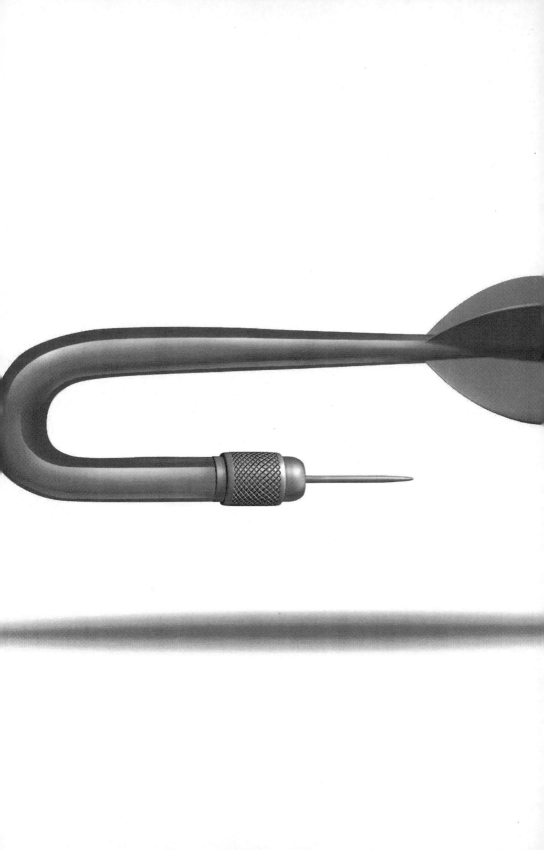

Four Resiliency Skills

AN OVERVIEW

Just as a car needs four wheels to more forward, there are four skills required to grow your resilient life: adaptability, agility, laugh-ability and alignment.

Chances are there's an app on your phone that tells you how to go from one location to another. It shows you whether traffic is moving, where there's a problem, and, if you know the area, how to get around an obstacle. We will do the same thing as we cultivate the skills of adaptability, agility, laugh-ability, and alignment.

I'll explain briefly the four skills and then flesh out your GPS actions and recalculating questions in successive sections.

SKILL 1: ADAPTABILITY

Adaptability is predicated on finding multiple responses to any given situation. It is foundational for resilience and literally rests upon our ability to challenge old ways of doing things, to actively seek different viewpoints, to beware of sacred cows, and to know that solutions can come from anywhere or anyone.

Courage comes into play when we own up to our own reluctance to look for personal and professional blind spots. The very person we don't want to listen to might be the very person with that one critical idea.

Adaptability also requires a change of heart, an ability to work on intelligent optimism, reframing what is possible rather than what is impossible. For example, a road crew drilling through a mountain discovered a fresh water spring. Such an occurrence can wreck havoc in trying to complete the road. However, this company decided to divert the spring and now sells bottled water while, at the same time, completing the road. That's reframing.

Pauline just lost her husband Bill, a brilliant nuclear physicist, who could not even form coherent sentences because of the ravages of Alzheimer's. Pauline's comment, "At least he is at peace and his brilliant brain might offer some clues for researchers." Reframing.

Adaptability is about thinking and feeling. Agility, on the other hand, is about action and movement.

SKILL 2: AGILITY

Agility is the ability to move quickly and easily. It implies nimbleness, flexibility, and speed. It is one thing to intellectually create multiple actions. It is another thing to move forward. Action is the antidote for anxiety.

The trick is to move wisely. Analysis paralysis might take over. Instead, the resilient individual and organization decide what small steps can gain a foothold. There's ample feedback while actions are taken. Rewards center on the willingness to act, to take risks, and to share results.

Action also looks at physical action. In short, care of the human body. Exercise, sleep, and nutrition demand attention in growing through challenge or opportunity. Sometimes, the greatest step one can take is to sleep. Refreshed, the mind has a better chance at being creative and innovative.

Sometimes, when faced with a feeling of powerlessness, doing anything that gives a sense of control can be immensely beneficial. One woman, when fired from her job of 30 years, created a networking group at her church of people looking for work. Another company, caught in the grip of the recession, pulled employees together to explore how costs could be cut without cutting people. Some employees volunteered to work part time so that those with less financial resources could continue working.

SKILL 3: LAUGH-ABILITY

Victor Borges said, *Laughter is the shortest distance between two people.* It is also the shortest distance between your brain and your body. The ability to find humor and generate a sense of playfulness actually increases creativity. Laughter separates the serious from the trivial, the trite from the tremendous.

In a Chilean mine disaster, against all odds, these men survived. Adaptability (multiple rescue methods and listening to many experts) and agility were paramount. They also

39

employed laugh-ability, or at least a way to keep a sense of humor about this very serious predicament. When a camera was lowered into the mine, one miner gave a tour of their surroundings, showing a table where they played cards and held meetings. At the end of the video, the trapped men burst into a hearty rendition of the national anthem. In short, the men took control where they could, added some spirit to the horror of being trapped, and—as a waiting world discovered, kept everyone alive until rescue. (You can read more about the resiliency lessons from this incident at the end of this book.)

Play belongs in the realm of laugh-ability. It was the jester of old who spoke the truth in a non-threatening way by using humor and play. Free-form play and improvisation not only break barriers but open up a world of potential ways to handle situations.

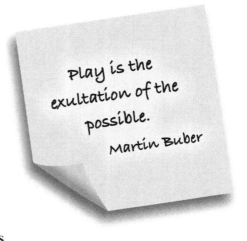

Play is the exultation of the possible.

Martin Buber

SKILL 4: ALIGNMENT

In 2008, I trekked a portion of the remote western Indian Himalayas, visiting villages as well as ancient monasteries. These still-standing structures, looking fragile in a terrain of rock and stone scoured by wind, rain and snows, have survived because of one thing: they are built on bedrock. The main buildings are lined up on the strongest part of the mountain.

To remain standing, humans too need bedrock. As Viktor Frankl stated, *Those who have a 'why' to live, can bear with almost any 'how'. (Man's Search for Meaning: Gift Edition)*. Resilient people and individuals have a reason greater than themselves for keeping on. Whether a child to raise, a song to sing, a book to write, or a community to protect, there is a sense that something or someone matters. That alignment guides adaptability.

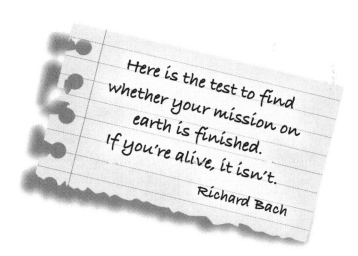

Here is the test to find whether your mission on earth is finished. If you're alive, it isn't.

Richard Bach

Adaptability:

HARNESS THE POWER OF MANY OPTIONS

It is good to have an end to a journey toward;
but it is the journey that matters in the end.

Ursula K. LeGuin

Re-imaging resiliency demands that we harness the power of many options. The more options we have for thinking and acting, the more powerful and energized we become.

You have described your current location when you set your GPS, describing current reality. Now it is time to question if your current location is where you want to stay.

Here are seven options to consider when developing the skill of adaptability.

OPTION 1: UNSTICK YOUR THINKING

What We Think Matters. How We Act Counts.

Where do you find yourself today—this place called your current location? In studying why some leaders and their organizations are not sustainable, I realized there is a possible unwillingness or an inability to clearly define one's current reality.

Perhaps you too have noticed that companies continue to ignore information, insist on actions without careful consideration, and in short—shoot themselves in the foot. And it has been going on for a LONG time. It's an illusion of knowledge.

> The greatest obstacle to discovering the shape of the continents and the oceans was not ignorance but the illusion of knowledge.
>
> Daniel Boorstin

» Consider the American automaker that sold cars in Japan with the driving column on the left side instead of the right.

» Consider the almost-flop of Euro Disney that insisted American food, no alcohol, and only English would be spoken at the French resort.

» Consider the famed Brentano's bookstore that closed because it refused to offer discount prices.

» Consider the demise of Kodak, the brick-and-mortar store Sharper Image, and Howard Johnson restaurants.

All were failures of thinking. It was not for lack of information. Rather, it was an unwillingness and possibly arrogance to believe that the world would never change or that there could be *many* answers instead of just one. Their current location would always remain the same. Stuck.

In short, they either didn't ask the right questions or they didn't like the answers they got. It continues to happen again and again because organizations are comprised of individuals.

In our personal lives, we also try to handle situations, events, challenges, or opportunities in the same way we have always handled them. Hunker down, do more of the same, and hope for a better result. We stay in our current location.

Consider *your* current location as common knowledge. This is the way you and the people around you think about a situation. It is the way everyone in your circle commonly responds. It's "the way we do things around here." It can be the family myth that you aren't to ask for help but just "pull yourself up by the bootstraps." It is "standard practice."

Think of your current location as patterned and formulaic. Consider this the corporate sacred cow, the institutional process that might have worked once upon a time but now keeps people from innovating and profits from growing.

In a 24/7 world where surprises are the new normal, where work and life can shift in a nanosecond, there's a great need to challenge current reality and common knowledge. *This is where the skill of adaptability comes into play.* We seek not just one more way of responding but MANY ways of responding. In biological terms, the word is requisite variety. Simply stated: *The organism with the greatest number of responses to any given situation is the one that will survive.*

We want to leave this current location and venture outward, thinking and creating as many options for ourselves as possible.

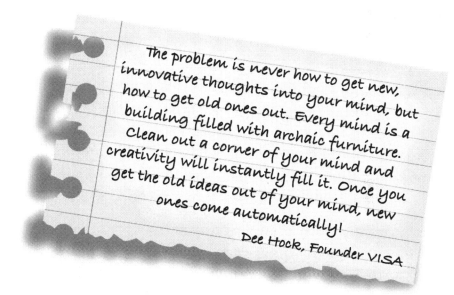

The problem is never how to get new, innovative thoughts into your mind, but how to get old ones out. Every mind is a building filled with archaic furniture. Clean out a corner of your mind and creativity will instantly fill it. Once you get the old ideas out of your mind, new ones come automatically!

Dee Hock, Founder VISA

Professional Example: It would be fair to say that in general, banks are staid institutions with the same type of general work: handling checking and savings accounts, managing monetary flow, investments, making smart loans, and liquidity… all of which makes banks look pretty much the same.

However, at Toronto Dominion Bank, officials decided to challenge the way things were done and look for creative opportunities to court and keep their customers. Think of this as **"presilience"— preemptive resiliency.**

According to Stan Phelps, President of 9 Inch Marketing, a firm that tracks customer experience, Toronto Dominion Bank broke out of the "common knowledge" with these innovations:

» Toronto Dominion Bank bases its philosophy on convenience. They are open 7 days and most nights until 8 p.m.

» Managers are taught to open the doors to the branch 10 minutes before the stated time… and this is key, keep the doors open until 10 minutes after the stated closing time.

» They find ways to connect with customers and show their appreciation for their business. There is the clever Penny Arcade that allows customers to exchange coins for dollars for free. They make this fun for kids by challenging them to guess the exact amount.

» They are pet and kid friendly, whether it's a green lollipop or dog biscuit.

» They purposefully try to eliminate barriers. Branches are all glass and the counters are extremely low.

» They believe in Branded Acts of Kindness. Doing the little things to thank customers, like creative Automated Thanking Machines. Watch their video at http://youtu.be/ bUkN7g_bEAI

PROFESSIONAL GPS ACTION

1. Define as much as you can about your current professional situation, process, and product.

2. In your presilience logbook, write your responses to the recalculating questions. Find someone with whom to have a conversation.

PROFESSIONAL RECALCULATING QUESTIONS

1. Do you operate under the premise: "The devil I know is better than the one I don't?"

2. Test the status quo. What is going on?

3. Why not change? Who says you can't?

4. What would happen if? Are you SURE?

5. What are the sacred cows that might bind your hands?

6. Can you practice "joyous anarchy" and explore other options?

7. Are you paying attention to core tasks in-house and contracting out other tasks?

8. What are the things you are doing today that if you were not already doing, you would not start doing? Why? Why not?

9. Was anything discarded that shouldn't have been? Was anything discarded which now is relevant?

10. Are you stuck in that uncomfortable "comfort" zone? Might you find being a victim more rewarding than being a victor? Let's face it... sympathy and consolation have their own rewards. Your energy will be depleted living

in that zone and colleagues and friends will move away. It's too energy-draining to be with "sad-sacks" over the long haul.

PERSONAL GPS ACTION

1. Do you operate under the premise: "The devil I know is better than the one I don't?"

2. Define as much as you can about your current personal situation.

3. In your presilience logbook, write your responses to the recalculating questions. Find someone with whom to have a conversation.

PERSONAL RECALCULATING QUESTIONS

1. Define as much as you can about your current situation.

2. What are the challenges? What are the opportunities?

3. What resources are on hand? Resources are not only financial or material, but also support people.

4. What is the worst thing that could happen? The best thing?

5. Ask "why" at least 5 times—fascinating exercise but each "why" brings you closer to reality.

6. How shall you divide up the information gathering? If there are others involved, who takes the lead?

7. How many options can you create for yourself? Even if you don't like all of them, listing them out carries great benefit.

8. Are you stuck in that uncomfortable "comfort zone?" Might you find being a victim more rewarding than being a victor? Let's face it… sympathy and consolation have their own rewards. Your energy will be depleted living in that zone and colleagues and friends will move away. It's too energy-draining to be with "sad-sacks" over the long haul.

And the day came when the risk to remain tight in the bud was more painful than the risk it took to blossom.

Anaïs Nin

SOME ROADBLOCKS THAT CAN GET YOU STUCK

If you are like the majority of humans (myself included), you might have looked at the answers you wrote to the aforementioned Recalculating Questions and proceeded to tell yourself things like:

» There's no way this will work.

» So-and-so will be against it.

» It costs too much money.

» There's not enough time.

» It really isn't THAT broken.

» I don't have the skill.

» Why bother? Things will change again—sometime.

» I'm just destined for a hard life.

» I've never done this before.

» Bad things come in threes—there's more around the bend.

You know the drill. Our monkey mind just chatters away, producing what researchers say is approximately 60,000 thoughts per day! It's that internal, infernal chatter that can so easily build up a wall of resistance. Amazingly, scientists also tell us that 95% of those thoughts are the same as yesterday! How many times have you found yourself ruminating over an issue—thoughts that play in circular fashion across your mind—particularly when you are trying to sleep?

Here's the kicker: *80% of those thoughts are negative!*

Now before you jump off a cliff in despair, consider this—it makes sense that our primitive brain would always be looking out for what could go wrong: wild animals, natural disaster, an enemy. Additionally we are THE ONLY species on the planet capable of projecting negative thoughts on a current or future event. No rosebush opened up and thought, *Darn, it's raining. I'm going to get mildew.* No dog ran up to its master thinking, *I sure hope he pets me because I have had a really bad day!* No Monarch butterfly shed its cocoon thinking, *I only have two weeks to live!*

No wonder resiliency is hard work. We need help filling the black hole of negativity.

OPTION 2: BEWARE OF RED ANTS

Years ago, my siblings and I took Joan, a relative, with us to explore the wonderful New England fall colors. Joan is a negative person. If you said, *It's the land of milk and honey,* she'd respond: *No it's not. It's calories and cholesterol.*

Just as we drove around a stunning part of the dirt road, my sister shouted out, *Wait. Stop the car! I must get out and take a photo of those amazing colors, the church steeple, and that bright New England sky.*

Within a heartbeat, Joan said, *Well, I hope she doesn't stand in red ants!*

Huh? Red ants?? Are you kidding me?? What an imagination!

Here's the scary thought: it might be genetic.

Only recently did I discover that Joan's red ants are referenced in papers on negativity. *ANTS: Automatic Negative Thoughts.*

GPS ACTION

1. Take steps against negativity.

2. Catch yourself when a negative thought or expression comes flying in your brain or out of your mouth. What did you say or think?

3. Can you flip it around into something positive? It's not easy to do and it often helps to have an optimistic partner who can help you alter the thought.

4. Just say it. Write it. Repeat it. You don't even have to believe it. What's fascinating is that our brains don't know the difference between fact and fiction. The more I feed my brain positive thoughts, the more I create a different roadway in my brain. I begin to behave differently.

5. In your presilience logbook, write your responses to the recalculating questions. Find someone with whom to have a conversation.

RECALCULATING QUESTIONS

1. Where are you envisioning the worst?

2. What are the REAL chances the "worst" will happen?

3. What can you tell yourself—even if you don't believe it—that could give you a more positive outcome?

If this last question sounds like California woo-woo, consider this:

When my stepdaughter was younger, we had a very difficult time. She and I tangled like skeins of yarn in a washing machine. I began to say to myself, before she got home from school: *I love you. I know you're having a hard time and I believe in you.*

Did I believe what I was saying at that time? Nope. But I kept putting that thought in my head. In short order, she began to behave better. I didn't change anything other than work on this very conscious thought.

I am not naïve. Affirmations can only take you so far. It takes willpower to catch yourself or your team being negative and seek a positive response. Consider that research shows willpower outperforms academic performance by a factor of two. What you desire to create can potentially overcome a lack of skill. You WILL figure it out.

What can help cultivate resiliency is this next action.

OPTION 3: PRACTICE INTELLIGENT OPTIMISM

> *A pessimist sees challenge in every opportunity. An optimist sees opportunity in every challenge.*
>
> Winston Churchill

Thanks to Dr. Martin Seligman, director of the Penn State Positive Psychology Center and author of numerous books including, *Authentic Happiness* and *Learned Optimism,* we now know that optimism can be learned. Seligman's research led the way to the positive psychology movement that has had a profound impact on resiliency, confidence, and courage.

Intelligent optimism is reframing an event, looking for other ways to describe what is happening. When my sister said I was experiencing, *AFGO: Another F%$^&& Growth Opportunity,* she reframed my life for me. When the space of "lost" is reframed as a "fertile void," there's a sense of wonder, adventure, and possibility. Think of this as looking for the "gift" in the "garbage."

Intelligent optimism can also evoke humor. Shelley Winters, a plus sized actress, declared that she was not overweight… just nine inches too short!

One of the finest examples of intelligent optimism occurred during the almost near disaster of a lunar landing by Apollo 13 in 1970. Everything that could go wrong went wrong: the landing was aborted after an oxygen tank exploded, crippling the Service Module. Power became limited; there was a loss of cabin heat, a shortage of potable water, and the critical need to jury-rig the carbon dioxide removal system. How could the crew ever be returned safely to earth?

Despair was running high with each attempt the ground engineers made. It looked like failure. However, Mission Control Commander Gene Kranz reframed the potential disaster telling the team, *This will be our finest hour!*

In fact, if you want a pick-me-up and a look at resilience in action, rent the historical docudrama, *Apollo 13,* starring Tom Hanks.

GPS ACTION

1. Get help from a trusted friend or family member if you need it. I'd love to know what you write. E-mail me Eileen@eileenmdargh.com.

2. In your presilience logbook, write your responses to the recalculating questions. Find someone with whom to have a conversation.

RECALCULATING QUESTIONS

1. Have you ever seen or heard of a similar situation what was successfully resolved?

2. What conditions made that possible and how could you re-create them?

3. Is your current situation permanent? Pervasive? Personal?

In considering the last question, be honest. Often, only one of these questions might be answered in the affirmative. However, negative responses can become so dramatic that they all seem true. Consider the teen who just broke up with her boyfriend. If she were like my teens, one would think her romantic life is permanently broke—that ALL of her life is ruined, and that it is personal. Only the latter *might* be true.

A Word About PTSD

Just as Dr. Seligman began the positive psychology movement, researchers are now tackling the growth responses related to severe trauma and loss. Richard Tedeschi, a psychologist, researcher, and a clinician at the University of North Carolina, Charlotte, and Lawrence Calhoun, a psychologist at U.N.C., started their research by interviewing survivors of severe injuries. They went on to survey older people who had lost their spouses or had been paralyzed. Person after person told them the same thing: they wished deeply that they had not lost a spouse or been paralyzed, but nonetheless, the experience changed them for the better.

In 1995, he and Calhoun coined the term PTG, or "Post-Traumatic Growth." Experiencing growth in the wake of trauma, Tedeschi asserts, PTG far more common than PTSD and can even coexist with it.

Finally, in 2008, under the persistent prodding of Brigadier General Rhonda Cornum and with input from Seligman, the military began a $125 million Army-wide program called Comprehensive Soldier Fitness. It is intended to help soldiers become more resilient and to help them recognize how the trauma of combat can change them for the better.

This is a specialized field of resiliency. Never have we had so many men and women returning to this nation bearing horrific wounds (both seen and unseen) from war. If you believe that your issues are due to severe trauma, I urge you to do more research and find help.

OPTION 4: TURN THE PAGE

There's a tendency to want things to "go back the way they were". Turning the page is both a mantra as well as a physical gesture that I teach to my audiences. It anchors the point in our brains and begins to create a new mental pattern. Every time you hear yourself say *"things aren't the way they use to be"*, *"there's too much change"*, or some such statement, take your dominant hand and gesture turning the page while you mutter the words, "TURN THE PAGE!"

GPS ACTION

1. Seek a turn-the-page buddy. Ask your buddy to call you on it whenever you moan for the past.

2. In your presilience logbook, write your responses to the recalculating questions. Find someone with whom to have a conversation.

RECALCULATING QUESTIONS

1. What are you holding on to and does it serve you now?

2. What do you value about the past and how can you bring it into the present?

OPTION 5: SEEK OTHERS' WISDOM

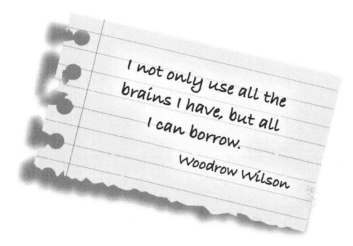

I not only use all the brains I have, but all I can borrow.

Woodrow Wilson

There's another way to increase options for being resilient, for moving toward our desired future. Like all good adventurers, we become seekers, finding out what others know that we don't. Who has walked this road before? What do others see that we do not? Our willingness to ask for information and help exponentially increases our adaptability—as long as we are willing to listen to other voices.

The first voice is the internal voice: Me, Myself, And I. It would be naïve if we didn't also admit that there are times when we are so confused that we can't even find the front door of our current location much less leave it. We need help! We need someone to reframe for us.

What my sister provided for me and what Gene Kranz offered his Mission Control team was a different viewpoint. I had to ask for input and so did the engineers.

Remember, to be optimally adaptable, you seek as many ways as possible to respond to a given opportunity or challenge.

What fascinates me is that we often fail to seek that input.

Sometimes, we're more concerned with looking good rather than being good and so we become masters at what Chris Argyris calls, "skilled incompetence". We become very adept at protecting ourselves from the sometimes-painful parts of learning and hesitant to say, *I don't know.*

Cognitive dissonance throws itself into high gear in this part of our journey. In short, once an idea is planted into a corporate or individual pattern, any data that contradicts that idea is discounted. Recall President Bush's insistence that there was no recession, despite poll after poll in which the public expressed grave concern. In too many instances, I've seen organizations survey employees and customers and then discount the results.

Management often fails to ask the right people for insight. Example: McDonald's in Great Britain learned the hard way when they launched a new sandwich of cheese, salad and pickle, dubbed

McPloughman's. When the menu item flopped, an investigation revealed that not even McDonald's employees liked the sandwich but nobody had asked his or her opinion beforehand.

On a personal level, we might not care for the person who is offering another view point or, we think, *What do THEY know about this situation?* How many of us ignored the view points of our parents, only to discover—years later—how smart they were?

GPS ACTION

1. Design a method for getting input from others. Face-to-face is always the best. Go to the people closest to and most impacted by the event.

2. Decide whose input matters to the health of the organization. Who will you ask?

3. In your presilience logbook, write your responses to the recalculating questions. Find someone with whom to have a conversation.

RECALCULATING QUESTIONS

1. Whose input do we resist and why? Might it be that cognitive dissonance is operating?

2. Seek what others know. What possibilities could result as a way of accepting some or all of this information?

3. Ask, *What might be true? How can I most effectively respond to this feedback? What needs to be changed based upon this information? What am I/we resisting and why?*

OPTION 6: SERVE ORANGE JUICE

Constructive criticism. Feedback. 360 degree assessments. We've all heard these terms as things that leaders do to help employees and high potentials.

But in this age of quick-hit twitter feeds, I wonder how many senior leaders ACTIVELY court and seek out input to help their own growth AND the growth of their organization.

Years ago, I had the opportunity to meet Tom Kilpatrick, then the head of training for USS POSCO, a steel operation in Northern California. Tom told me of being sent to replace the commander of a Navy ship in the South Seas. The commander had been removed "for cause." The ship had the highest number of pending disciplinary cases for that class of ship in the Navy AND the lowest rates of retention.

Yikes. What a tough assignment. But at the end of two years, those numbers were reversed.

I asked Tom what he did.

I served orange juice, he said with a smile.

OK, I am often not the brightest light bulb in the box so I asked him to explain.

He said that in the first week of his command, he was in his bunk at night pondering how to turn the men around.

Tom thought... *What is the most miserable place to be on this ship, in the middle of the night, in the South Seas? The engine room!*

He got up. Went to the galley, got glasses, and orange juice and went into the engine room.

Hey guys. I thought you'd need something cool. Now tell me... what do we need to do down here to make this the best engine room in the Navy?

Think about it. He showed up where he was least expected. He came as a servant leader bearing a gift. He asked a question and he listened intently.

By morning, that story had spread like wildfire. He said it brought him more loyalty than any action he might have taken.

Think about it. He couldn't grow the command if he didn't know. He constantly sought input. He actively listened. He responded.

Where do you need to go to serve orange juice?

GPS ACTION

1. In your presilience logbook, make a list of people to whom you might "serve orange juice."

2. In your presilience logbook, write your responses. Find someone with whom to have a conversation.

RECALCULATING QUESTIONS

1. What open-ended question might supply you with insights you might never have? Begin your questions with these words: who, what, when, where, why, and how.

2. When will you contact them? How will you do that? I suggest that if face-to-face is not possible, at least make telephone contact. Email is never conducive to fully fleshed conversation.

OPTION 7: SEEK A WISDOM CIRCLE

Consider forming a Wisdom Circle. To form a Wisdom Circle, gather a number of trusted friends around you. Briefly state what you are grappling with. Then be quiet. You are there to seek out their insight and their wisdom. You are *not* there to respond one way or another. It's up to you as to what you do with that information or input.

Master activist teacher Parker Palmer calls this a "Clearness Committee." Look at http://www. couragerenewal.org/parker/writings/ clearness-committee/.

Started in the 1600s by Quakers, the Clearness Committee is a practice that believes each of us has an inner wisdom, a teacher, a voice of truth that can offer guidance. However, that voice is often garbled by our insecurities, confusions, fears, or critical others. A Clearness Committee helps you uncover answers within yourself.

Read Chapter VIII, "Living the Questions," in Parker's book *A Hidden Wholeness: The Journey Toward an Undivided Life* (San Francisco: Jossey-Bass Publishers, 2009). There you will find detailed, step-by-step guidance, as well as a DVD with footage of Parker teaching the process to a group.

GPS ACTION

1. Ask yourself who has been in a similar situation and if you'd feel comfortable asking their advice. Just because you ask doesn't mean you are compelled to use their input. Write their names and contact information in your logbook.

2. Decide which people you would like to call first—perhaps for a cup of coffee or a meal.

3. In conversation, empty your mind of preconceived answers. Take in without judgment.

4. Follow up later with not only a thank you but what you did with their input. People like to know they have helped, even in some small way.

5. Seek professional help from a counselor, a member of your clergy, or a trusted physician.

6. Read books related to your current state. When we called in hospice to help with Mom, I needed to understand all I could about what was happening and how to help her. I discovered a wealth of first hand information

as well as spiritual viewpoints that gave me more options with which to understand the final passage of life.

7. In your presilience logbook, write your responses to the recalculating questions. Find someone with whom to have a conversation.

RECALCULATING QUESTIONS

1. What is the situation for which you would like clarity?

2. What specifically would make this Wisdom Circle most valuable?

Agility:

SPRING INTO ACTION

The best thing you can do is the right thing;
the next best thing you can do is the wrong thing;
the worst thing you can do is nothing.

Theodore Roosevelt

S o far, everything we've explored has to do with identifying what your current location looks like (current reality, common knowledge, the "NOW") and finding multiple options. Now, it is time to take a risk. Action is the antidote for anxiety. Agility is about mental, emotional, and physical hardiness.

Here are seven actions to consider when developing the skill of agility.

ACTION 1: CONTROL THE CONTROLLABLE

We lose our way and become discouraged when we attempt to "take on more than we can chew." We attempt to control something that is truly out of our control.

Example: Recently I was asked to create a resiliency webinar for college counselors and one of the stated objectives was to create an educational environment that fosters resilience. My question to this request was: *Just how much control do counselors have over creating such an environment?* The answer: *Not much.* They are not in the classroom, in the dorm, and students only come to them on an as-needed basis.

Does that render them helpless? NO! What if the counselors held focus groups in dorms to talk about issues? What if they created (with some students)

YouTube videos that looked at the stress of college life and how to handle it? What if they held training sessions with dorm monitors to help them identify at-risk kids? What if they did informal faculty briefings?

Get the picture? Counselors can't control the college environment BUT, within their sphere of influence, they can offer assistance.

I call this the Earthquake Litmus Test. I live in California. Earthquakes will occur. I can't control an earthquake BUT I do have actions I can take:

» Move from the state (an option but I want to stay married to my sweet California-fanatic husband).

» I can make sure I have all the emergency supplies ready.

» I can have a detailed "plan" for all family members so we know what to do.

» I can take first aid classes.

(Note: Think of these options as **"presilience"** preemptive resilience or proactive resilience.)

GPS ACTION

1. Clearly write or talk about the desired outcome and then ask for volunteers to be involved in crafting action. Why volunteers? When faced with challenge or opportunity, you want people who are already committed to moving forward. This is no time to have nay-sayers.

2. Break actions into small pieces.

3. Create a short feedback loop. Nothing will sap your resilient spirit than proceeding full steam ahead and finding out six months later that it did not work.

4. Reward effort. If an action did not work, cheer on the person who at least tried and then sought out alternatives if it did not work. (Ben & Jerry's Ice Cream has a graveyard complete with headstones—for flavors that did NOT work. Very funny and also encourages risk taking.)

5. Create an action plan that begins with some of the easier things to accomplish. Being able to see results–even if small—boosts your spirit.

6. In your presilience logbook, write your responses to the recalculating questions. Find someone with whom to have a conversation.

RECALCULATING QUESTIONS

1. What are you trying to control?

2. Do you really have the power? The authority? The resources?

3. What can you REALLY control?

4. What are three easy-steps you can take now, beginning today to grow your resiliency?

5. Who could be your action buddy—someone who will check in with you to see if you did the one or two things you set out to do?

6. What are you afraid of? Face what you fear and lean into it! On an expedition to the western Indian Himalayas, we had to cross white-water rivers on foot. Very terrifying. I discovered that if I pushed my body into the oncoming white water, I was actually much stronger.

Remember: ACT Is More Powerful Than Re-Act

ACTION 2: CELEBRATE SMALL WINS

After 9/11, an incident happened at LAX Airport. The canine squad came and once things had cleared up, I struck up a conversation with one of the dog handlers. He informed me that while doing the rescue effort after the Towers collapsed, the dogs would become discouraged if they didn't find someone.

When this happened, the handlers took turns, lightly covering up one of their team so that the dog could have a sense of accomplishment when it found someone. This made such an impression on me. If a dog needs encouragement when the going is tough, how much more do humans need?

If you are part of a team going through difficult times, find ways to celebrate small wins. Whether it's giving someone a stuffed salmon because he swam upstream against all odds or taking time out to high five and whistle when another effort succeeded, acknowledging effort always wins the day.

GPS ACTION

1. Make it a daily practice to find someone to reward. It can be as simple as saying "Thank you."

2. In your presilience logbook, write your responses to the recalculating questions. Find someone with whom to have a conversation.

RECALCULATING QUESTIONS

1. What small wins can you reward yourself for accomplishing?

2. What have others done that you need to reward?

3. Can you make your reward something YOU see on a daily basis so you are reminded of progress?

By the way—I do mean small. When I realized I needed to work on my physical stamina, I rewarded myself with fancy stickers in my date book each time I exercised. I started that practice probably 20 years ago and still keep it up! This is why I believe so firmly in the next action item.

ACTION 3: EXERCISE TO ENERGIZE

When work and life seem to spin out of control, the fastest way to know that aliens haven't hijacked you is to take control of your physical body.

Exercise pumps up the healing power of your brain's feel-good neurotransmitters called endorphins.

Aerobic activity of ANY intensity sends blood coursing through your body, firing off synapses in your nervous system and brain. Such activity actually lowers stress levels and—when compared with the couch potato who says, *I am too tired,* those stress levels stay down far longer.

Exercise improves your mood. Regular exercise can increase self-confidence and lower the symptoms associated with mild depression and anxiety.

GPS ACTION

1. Write down at least 2 physical exercises you believe you can commit to doing.

2. In your presilience logbook, write your responses to the recalculating questions. Find someone with whom to have a conversation.

RECALCULATING QUESTIONS

1. What would help you keep this commitment to exercise?

2. How will you reward yourself for each time your exercised?

3. Do you need an exercise buddy? If so, who will you ask?

ACTION 4: PRACTICE MINDFULNESS

When introduced at the University of MA, Medical School in 1979 by Jon Kabat-Zinn, few could have known that this practice of mindfulness would become mainstream in major business schools and global organizations.

Mindfulness is basically slowing down, breathing deeply, and maintaining a moment-by-moment awareness of thoughts, feelings, bodily sensations, and surrounding environment.

Study after study has shown the physical and mental benefits of mindfulness in general and it has even become formulized as MBSR (Mindfulness-Based Stress Reduction).

According to the University of CA Berkeley publication, *The Greater Good*:

» Mindfulness is good for our bodies: A seminal study found that, after just eight weeks of training, practicing mindfulness meditation boosts our immune system's ability to fight off illness.

» Mindfulness also helps our minds. Several studies have found that mindfulness increases positive emotions while reducing negative emotions and stress. Indeed, at least one study suggests it may be as good as antidepressants in fighting depression and preventing relapse.

» Mindfulness changes our brains. Research has found that it increases density of gray matter in brain regions linked to learning, memory, emotion regulation, and empathy.

You don't have to move to a monastery or sit in a lotus position to practice mindfulness. Give yourself five minutes to breathe in to the count of four and out to the count of six. Just pay attention to the moment. That's all. My clients tell me they feel much calmer and more centered in their day and better able to grow through whatever is in the present moment.

At the start of an intense two-day management retreat with senior executives who had flown into India from around the globe, I decided to introduce them to mindfulness. It was optional. To my delight, all but one person showed up. For 45 minutes, we laid on yoga mats around a pool while a mindfulness teacher guided us. Many of the executives later expressed appreciation for adding that dimension to their world.

Make mindfulness a practice in the morning before jumping out of bed. Breathe. You have been given the gift of a new day.

End your day with mindfulness. Again, just breathe. Calm down. Do not read your email, text message or anything else. You are entering a time of rest. Don't fill your mind with activity. Just breathe as you turn off the light.

To read more http://greatergood.berkeley.edu/topic/mindfulness/definition

GPS ACTION

1. Make a commitment to begin and end each day with at least 3 minutes of mindfulness— deep breathing. No talking. Just breathe.

2. In your presilience logbook, write your responses to the recalculating questions. Find someone with whom to have a conversation.

RECALCULATING QUESTIONS

1. What will you need to do to keep this commitment?

2. How will you learn more about mindfulness?

ACTION 5: CONSIDER FAITH

Along the resiliency journey, faith serves as a hiking pole to steady the course. It has been described as a belief in things yet unseen. Despite all evidence to the contrary, the resilient spirit KNOWS that "this too shall pass." The resilient person KNOWS that despite the gloom of challenges or the trepidation of major events, the dawn eventually breaks through.

Faith is the bird that sings when the dawn is still dark.

Tagore

Unfortunately, it's one thing to "know" and another thing to act on it. Perhaps this is why the writings of major religions all have variations of the phrase: *Do not be afraid.* It is found 356 times alone in the Bible. Everyone needs constant reassurance.

There is no action any of us take wherein we know—with 100% certainty—what will result. We walk out on faith all the time—we just don't think about it.

When we found the last hospice for Mom, we went on our instinct that this hospice would be a good match for Mom. The match was uncanny: a nurse, who was born in Pennsylvania, flew a plane, lived in Miami, and was a practicing Catholic. All of those attributes paralleled Mom!

GSP ACTION:

1. Look for a book, a YouTube video, or some article about an individual who thrived despite all odds. What can it teach you about faith? By the way, faith does not necessarily mean religion.

2. In your presilience logbook, write your responses to the recalculating questions. Find someone with whom to have a conversation.

RECALCULATING QUESTIONS

1. What is one action you could take now—a small one—that you know would be an act of faith?

2. What is the best thing that can happen?
    The worst thing?

Even if it doesn't turn out 100% perfectly, the knowledge you gain will bring you that much closer to a better action

ACTION 6: PRACTICE FORGIVENESS

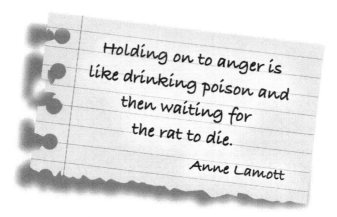

Holding on to anger is like drinking poison and then waiting for the rat to die.

Anne Lamott

You've been laid low. Brought to almost ruin. You've lost precious people, resources and time. Promises weren't kept. Lies were told. Perhaps even your reputation has been blackened. You don't just get mad. You yearn to get even.

Stop! That's a vicious spiral that only generates more negative energy and holds disastrous results. Don't believe me? Believe engineers who build bridges over water.

When a wave strikes a bridge, it sends out an energy field that is mirrored back to the bridge. Engineers design structures strong enough to sustain that second strike which can weaken the supports.

Wave theory. Works with human energy too. Send out negative energy. It will come crashing back to you.

There's a gift somewhere in every relationship and event. Find it and then say, *I forgive.*

GPS ACTION

1. Determine if you are holding on to a grudge or anger and what that feeling does for your spirit.

2. Write a letter (which you will NOT send) to this person and get the emotion out of your head/heart and on to paper.

3. Have a ritual and burn or bury that paper. Turn the page. Done. Next.

4. In your presilience logbook, write your responses to the recalculating questions. Find someone with whom to have a conversation.

RECALCULATING QUESTIONS

1. How would you feel if this event would vanish like smoke?

2. Does it serve you to hold on to this anger or grudge? Could it be holding you back?

3. What lessons in how you behave might be learned from this?

4. Do you think the other person is holding onto resentment?

5. What would it mean to you to take a higher road?

ACTION 7: NURTURE YOUR PIT CREW

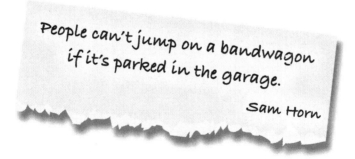

People can't jump on a bandwagon if it's parked in the garage.

Sam Horn

Who cheers you on at the finish line? Particularly if you come in last!

When things don't go as planned, when dark clouds gather, when others seem to grab the gold ring and you're holding an iron bauble, you need a pit crew. It might be a crew of one but that one is the world to you and visa versa.

Honor that pit crew. Let words of gratitude come from your mouth.

How strengthening it is to tell your pit crew how much their steadfast faith in you means everything.

There was a time when I couldn't find traction… A month in which the seeds I had planted were washed away by economic decisions. A month in which "everyone" seemed to have it together and I found parts of me falling off.

I bet I am not the only one who has been in this place. It was hard and dark. It was a drought brought about, in part, by external forces I couldn't control and my internal /infernal chatter would not turn off even if it SHOULD.

Not having much luck there.

My pit crew stepped in: my precious husband, my sister and brother, my neighbor, and my right-hand assistant. Each offered something for which I was so grateful.

I was so glad that month was over. I wanted to fall in love again with what I did and whom I did it for. February was the perfect time.

GPS ACTION

1. In your presilience logbook, write your responses. Find someone with whom to have a conversation.

RECALCULATING QUESTIONS

1. What are the names of your pit crew?

2. If you don't have one, how will you get one?

3. Whom do you want in it?

Sometimes, your crew might even include someone who is no longer living but in your imagination. You KNOW what they would say to help you.

ACTION 8: IMPROVISE TO STRATEGIZE

I am a firm believer that at some point we all must go to the college MSU—Making Stuff Up. When you can't figure out what action to take try something—*anything*. As long as you keep the action on a short leash with a short feedback loop and it's neither illegal nor immoral… proceed!

Example: My husband and I were part of a management team that had been awarded a major government contract. Tension was high as we beat out the incumbent contractor with the 750-page RFP I wrote. We were not greeted with open arms except by the employees on base who really did not like working for that contractor.

We were regarded with suspicion and—as if to challenge us even more—given an incredibly short time frame to turn the MWR (Morale Welfare & Recreation) components around. We needed all the resiliency and energy we could muster—and it had to be conveyed to some 250 plus employees in a matter of three weeks.

The answer: Strawberries.

You see, during our intake interviews, we found out from many of the employees that they were constantly kept in the dark, treated poorly, and talked down to.

We're like mushrooms, one manager told me. *And you know what mushrooms are covered with!*

Some angel on my shoulder must have opened my mouth because I heard myself say, *We believe in strawberries. They only grow in bright light and each berry is part of an integrated entire plant.*

That was it. All of us wore strawberry pins. We published a fast newspaper called "Strawberry Shorts" with each department talking about their new vision. The goal was to have everyone market and talk about all the base community functions—boosting up each other.

That improvisation became something that none of us would have dreamt possible—a desired future we could not have imagined.

Embedded in that strawberry story are the last two resiliency skills: laugh-ability and alignment. These skills are what makes the journey meaningful and dare I say, even fun.

GPS ACTION

1. Think of a situation that confounds you now. What can you do that is radically different? You might need some creative brains on this one.

2. In your presilience logbook, write your responses to the recalculating questions. Find someone with whom to have a conversation.

RECALCULATING QUESTIONS

1. What is humorous about the situation? How can you expand on it, exaggerate, and make it even funnier? (You'll know more when you read the next chapter.)

2. What type of story would you tell about this situation: drama, western, comedy, adventure?

3. Who can you involve in your improv? How will you introduce the "scene" and then invite your partners to jump in and be spontaneous? The first rule of improv is "accept what is given." This means you don't correct or alter what your partner says. Stay open to new ideas.

Laugh-ability:

LAUGH! PLAY! A LOT!!!

With the fearful strain that is on me night and day, if I did not laugh I should die.

Abe Lincoln.

f you know even half the story of Abraham Lincoln, you know this was a man who faced significant challenges as well as opportunities and managed to go through and grow through them all. His humor was legendary.

"Laugh-ability" is my made-up word for the good sense to try and find some way to spin an event so that you find something to laugh about—no matter how small.

In the last two years of my mother's life, she waged an uphill and then downhill battle with dementia and assorted physical conditions. One minute up. One minute down. We called her Yo-Yo Ma. It brought a smile to her face, made other people laugh, and spoke truthfully of the reality we faced.

Even as I write this, another friend is watching her mother go through the same journey. Lulu has given her Mom the feminine variation, "Lazarena" from the biblical character of Lazarus who was brought back from death.

When faced with the death of a loved one, humor can aid some of the grief. I remember reading about the death of a man who owned a fireworks factory. His instructions for his ashes: *Put them in the fireworks and shoot me off into the sky.* I would say that he went out with a bang!

My sister decided to scatter her husband's ashes in the many places they had vacationed. Unfortunately when she arrived in Africa, her luggage was missing. One week later when it was finally returned, everything was intact except for the small plastic bottle that held some of his ashes. Susan said her husband, Noam Pitlik, an Emmy award winning comedy director, would be heartily laughing at the thought that someone would be sniffing his ashes instead of cocaine!

Resiliency requires energy. Laughter is high wattage and better than gas!

Okay, you can take that last line anyway you want it. After all, this section is about humor.

A number of years ago, we took our granddaughter to Orlando and trudged through all four of the Walt Disney theme parks. Just when you thought you couldn't go on anymore, some Disney character or some exhibit would make us laugh or smile and we found more energy to go on.

Walt Disney World has capitalized on the idea of using laughter as a way of stimulating tired patrons around the park.

In fact, the Disney show Monster Inc. offered amazing creativity with animated and costumed monsters who were all looking to create energy to run their "city." But as monsters, they insisted that laughter produced more energy than screams!

I love that thought.

Through some hidden camera, they would pick out people in the audience and then talk about them in such a way that gales of laughter ensued. We loved it when my husband Bill was named, "That guy with the scary Hawaiian shirt." Frankly, some of his shirts *are* scary and funny!

Laughter produces more energy than screams.

GPS ACTION

1. In your presilience logbook, feel free to plug in anything that makes you laugh: one-liners, cartoons, jokes. Whatever.

2. Task yourself and possibly those around you to share one humorous thing.

3. In your presilience logbook, write your responses to the recalculating questions. Find someone with whom to have a conversation.

RECALCULATING QUESTIONS

1. What is funny about your current situation?

2. Where might others find humor?

3. What can you (or someone else) do to lighten the mood?

ENTER THE WORLD OF PLAY: A KISSING COUSIN TO LAUGH-ABILITY

The opposite of play is not work. It's depression. So states psychiatrist Stuart Brown in his new book, *Play: How It Shapes the Brain, Opens the Imagination and Invigorates the Soul.*

Brown has conducted more than 6,000 play studies on what goes wrong when people do not play—studying everything from serial killers to career-driven CEOs. Given the current plethora of economic turmoil, negative news, layoff paranoia, and growing unemployment lines, the notion of taking time to play sounds like a childish daydream. But if Brown is right, we could become a nation of stress-filled, hypertensive individuals who suffer far more than we need to and—at the very extreme—become downright dangerous to ourselves and others.

Brown is not original in his assertion. Anacharsis, a 6th BCE philosopher insisted that we are to *Play so that you may be serious.* Even in the Hellenistic world, play gave rise to scientists, writers, philosophers, and builders of great civilizations.

If you consider that the task before us is to build rebuild our cities, our enterprises, and our global community, then play becomes the non-chemical stimulant for channeling stress into productive outputs.

Play takes many forms. The trick is to find one that resonates with you. Consider these examples:

» Marc, a job-hunting, highly skilled communications expert in the entertainment field, coaches lacrosse when he's not interviewing. He appears more calm and confident since he started helping youngsters succeed in his favorite sport.

» Glenna, a recent widow and entrepreneur, has started dance lessons and added Bible study to her spare time. Her laugh comes easier now and she's discovering new ventures for her skill.

» Tom, faced with early retirement, collects Japanese postcards from the 1900s.

» Neil, the CEO of a consulting company, goes to an organic farm and helps his wife prepare scrumptious vegan meals.

» Eunice, a vice president in an international organization rides her Icelandic horse at every opportunity.

» And a president named Obama unwinds with a game of hoops. Certainly no other leader in modern time has had to face so many internal and external challenges and yet he finds time to play!

Think of these examples and you'll note that play is as much as a state of mind as it is an activity. It is a mental release that reduces stress levels in the body and engages the brain in a totally different type of thinking.

GPS ACTION

1. Give yourself permission to play. Put a play date with yourself on the calendar and treat it as sacred, like meeting with your most important client. Remind yourself that you'll be refreshed and thinking more clearly if you play.

2. Find the play that best suits you. Start a Play Diary, writing down moments of well-being.

It might be times you remember. It might be something that occurred during the week. It might be as simple as walking the dog or as complex as taking an eco-adventure tour. It might be a romantic night with your best beloved or a sweaty 100-mile bike ride. Whatever it is—in the doing, you feel a sense of contentment and joy.

3. Pass play along. Encourage others. Make sure you're not the driver who keeps employees chained to their desks but rather, lead the way. If you're in a position to do so, create a Fun Friday where everyone takes a turn at coming up with something that evokes joy, laughter, and contentment. One organization forbade email on Fridays between anyone in the building. Instead, messages were sent via paper airplanes.

4. Martin Buber, German Jewish biblical scholar, believed that, *Play is the exultation of the possible.* Isn't that what we all are looking for now—what is possible?

5. In your presilience logbook, write your responses to the recalculating questions. Find someone with whom to have a conversation.

RECALCULATING QUESTIONS

1. When was the last time you played?

2. What is keeping your from it? Does someone need to give you permission?

3. Can you memorize this line?

   Don't take life so seriously.
   Nobody comes out of it alive.

Along the journey to cultivating resiliency skills, rest and renewal are balm to your spirit. I found this article about a man who runs a fishing boat in Mexico. One of his customers offered a great notion about renewal.

KNOW WHAT STITCHES YOUR SOUL

Journey to La Paz, Mexico and you'll find the equivalent of fisherman's wharf where for at least 10 months out of the year, the hubbub of eating, drinking and—of course fishing—pulsate and predominate.

I only know these things because my husband adores traveling south, finding a panga and a "captain" to take him out into the Sea of Cortez. He also reads *Western Outdoor News* and the column "Baja Beat" written by Jonathan Roldan, owner/ operator of Tailhunters, a charter fishing company.

Running this fishing business and a restaurant gives Roldan the clout to write anything he darn well pleases about the area.

And pleased I was to read one of his columns that detailed the crazy, hectic, demanding pace of being a restaurateur, boat captain, customer service rep, baggage handler, fish packer, gear hauler, language translator, trade show vendor, marketer, and columnist.

The fireman from Oregon caught him flatfooted. It wasn't just the big beefy handshake and the thank-you that stopped him in his tracks. No, it was the gentle explanation of gratitude that took his breath away.

I really appreciate being here with you and Jill. This place stitches my soul.

Huh? Stitches his soul?

I'm a fireman. I see a lot of things. For a few days each year, being here in Baja help put my soul back together… Things start to make sense. It's my happy place. It helps me do what I do the rest of the year. Thanks, man.

Stitches my soul! What a powerful, simple concept. What a lesson for all of us as we charge forward to conquer mountains, slay dragons, deal with deadlines, fight the competition, care for aging parents, answer too many emails and become twitchy from too much Twitter.

Resiliency would be impossible without finding that happy place for renewal and restoration. It might be an hour in the garden or scanning the blue waters off Baja for a surface-slumbering sailfish. It might be playing with children or losing yourself in dance. When was the last time that you took out the proverbial needle and thread and paused? What stitches your soul?

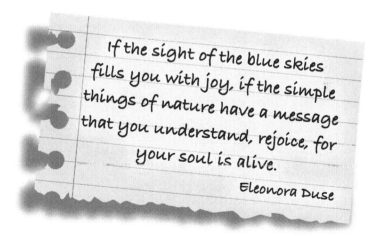

If the sight of the blue skies fills you with joy, if the simple things of nature have a message that you understand, rejoice, for your soul is alive.

Eleonora Duse

Not only can play and laughter stitch your soul, but it also promotes resiliency in others, offers a tool for innovation, and sparks hope among survivors.

For resiliency in others, consider Superheroes for kids in a hospital. A culture of enthusiasm and innovation generates tremendous care and attention to patients. That is exactly what Children's Hospital of Pittsburgh had in mind when they hired superheroes to "fight grime" off the windows of their pediatric wing. *We donned Spider-Man costumes and we rappelled down the side of the buildings,* said Harold Connolly, president of Highrise Window Cleaning of Clearwater, FL.

As a tool for innovation, consider Stand Up Planet, a new comedy documentary backed by the Bill and Melinda Gates Foundation. The documentary aims to change the global conversation about poverty by featuring comedians from countries such as India and South Africa.

To spark hope, consider survivor Allena Hansen who was attacked by a California black bear. The bear had torn away her jaw, lips, ear lope, and laid open her forehead. Doctors managed to not only save her face but her eyes as well. With over 1,000 stiches, the bear claw scar is living proof of the horrific event, but she uses humor to explain it.

I was kissed by bear lips. Watched that bugger spit my teeth out. But I am still beautiful with these hard-earned trophies.

She's finding meaning and reframing the issue of scars which is vital to coping with loss. Allena has started an online community to share blogs about traumatic incidents—but she blogs with humor.

GPS ACTION

1. Determine what stitches your soul.

2. Look on the Internet to find people who have used humor to deal with challenge. Don't be afraid to share one (not hundreds) with colleagues.

3. In your presilience logbook, write your responses to the recalculating questions. Find someone with whom to have a conversation.

RECALCULATING QUESTIONS

1. What can you do to bring a smile or a laugh to customers, clients, family members, and/ or neighbors?

2. What is stopping you? What might be the benefit to you?

Alignment:

STAND ON BEDROCK

One day your life will flash before your eyes.
Make sure it's worth watching.

Anon

Superhero window washers, Stand Up Planet comedians, and Allena Hansen are examples of people demonstrating the final resiliency skill: alignment.

These are folks who have connected and aligned with a purpose greater than a single event and as such, demonstrated soulfulness. You can see what values are core to them and get a sense of their mission.

Alignment played a huge role when we were awarded the government contract to manage and staff the MWR function and used "strawberries" as our theme. We had a value about honoring the dignity and talent of all our employees. Also, if we could create a viable series of MWR programs, we would then have developed community services that also honor the men and women in uniform and their families. It was never about the money—it was about what we could create that was bigger than all of us.

Think of this as leveraging your legacy. The clearer you become on your values and purpose, the more likely you are to grow through challenge or opportunity. Your work is not over.

GPS ACTION

1. Write a personal mission statement. Even if you are reading this for organizational

reasons, a personal mission statement becomes a litmus test for many actions and decisions. It lets you monitor your life's course, acting like an internal GPS. There's a corporate mission but equally important, you have a personal mission.

2. In your presilience logbook, write your responses to the recalculating questions. Find someone with whom to have a conversation.

RECALCULATING QUESTIONS

1. Imagine that your soul has left your body but you can still hear what people are saying about you. What do you hear? What do you want to hear? If you have children, what do they say?

2. Think of 2 people whom you admire and who inspire you. What about them inspires you? What traits do you admire?

3. If money were no object, after you had all the fun you wanted and paid whatever you wanted in bills, what would you do?

4. How would you know, each day, if you were living your mission?

Remember, this isn't the Ten Commandments and chiseled in stone. It can grow and change as you grow and change.

Putting it All Together:

TWO STORIES

WHAT TO DO WITH MOM

Confusion, anger and bitterness were Mom's responses when we realized that we had to take charge. She could no longer live by herself. We had tried other options like a visiting nurse but Mom refused to let her in. We asked for advice from neighbors and church members, social service folks, and looked at housing options in Florida.

Nothing seemed to work. Our decision was to move Mom to my house in California while she could still make some sense of what was happening and enjoy life. We sought advice from geriatric professionals on how to make transitions.

The miracle of synchronicity had placed three women in my road: the executive director of an assisted living community two miles from me, a geriatric nurse, and a specialist skilled in identifying elder needs. (What are the odds that I find that trio on the trek at some 15,000 feet in the Himalayas?)

We three had to act fast. While I transformed the back bedroom into a living space that had "her things" on the walls and bed, my siblings and our spouses jumped in to handle the move.

Once here, we used songs, rummy Q, trips to flower gardens, and lots of great food to evoke smiles and laughter from Mom. At the end of three months, a place opened up for Mom and within one week of that move she was saying how beautiful everything was. She felt loved, cared for, and, best of all, could see my sister and me frequently.

Mom got what she valued most: independence (although very structured) and her children. We got what we valued: a sense of caring for Mom through the rest of her life, making sure she was safe, cared for, surrounded by beauty and music, and loved beyond measure.

Notice the four skills in action:

» Adaptability to explore as many options as possible.

» Agility to put plans into action.

» Laugh-ability to create joy and play and smiles.

» Alignment to operate in a way consistent with our deeply held values.

RESILIENCY ROLE MODEL

There are countless stories of men and women, cities, even nations that I could cite as resiliency models. I chose this story because it has both a personal and a professional dimension. You will see both individuals and an "organization" undergoing significant (and life-threatening) change. You will read how a great leader held the "organization" together. You will see the four skills coming into play: adaptability, agility, laugh-ability and alignment.

You will learn how they control the controllable, celebrate small wins, and discover and use each person's individual strengths.

RESILIENCY LESSONS FROM CHILEAN MINE TRIUMPH

A worldwide web of viewers watched 33 miners being pulled to the surface following a 600,000 ton cave-in that happened nearly one-half mile below the ground on a barren plain in southern Chile. Besides showcasing the tenacity of rescuers and the miracle of technology, the miners themselves offer dramatic lessons in resiliency that can teach everyone.

Lesson 1: Hope relies on possibility not certainty. Shift foreman Luis Urzua practiced intelligent optimism when he reframed the event and steadfastly refused to give up. He maintained his leadership position and convinced the miners to eat only once every 48 hours. They kept that up for 17 days. Without optimism, it could have been anarchy in that dark hole. When the probe reached the men, Urzua's note that came to the surface expressed that hope: *We* *are fine in the shelter, the 33 of us.* This is not a note of desperation but one of optimism.

Lesson 2: Action is the antidote to anxiety. The miners stayed busy, continually clearing away rubble, monitoring gas levels, praying, and using the materials and medicine that eventually were sent down the shafts. In short, they controlled what they could control.

Lesson 3: Play to your strengths. Reports indicate that different men served different roles. Victor Rojas kept a logbook throughout the ordeal and became the writer who sent updates to the rescuers. Yonni Rojas used his experience in nursing to serve as the chief paramedic. Mario Heredia and Jose Gonzalez became the spiritual leaders, with Mario even requesting that a crucifix be sent down so he could erect a shrine. Edison Villaroel led the group in song, requesting that Elvis Presley songs be sent down. Imagine Elvis the Pelvis gyrating more than a half-mile into the earth!

Lesson 4: Laughter lightens the load. Surely bringing a load of rocks to the surface as a memento for rescuers showed a sense of humor. Sing-alongs, as described by reporters, did not appear to be funeral dirges.

Lesson 5: Faith can move mountains. Many of these miners expressed a deep religious conviction through their Catholic faith. Faith, however, is not the sole property of one religious group. To have a sense of a power beyond one's human limitations is to tap into a wellspring of confidence and courage.

Lesson 6: Don't bounce back. Grow forward. After 69 days, many of the miners expressed finding another side to themselves and their lives. Changed men rose from the earth, men who vowed to live differently. Whether marrying a long-time girlfriend, finding new comfort in family, or advocating for changes in mining operations, each of the 33 now have the possibility for becoming better through this ordeal.

So it is for all who face events that might seem as dark and crushing as what happened on a cold day in Copiapó, Chile. The lessons offered by 33 miners might spark a chord to help many discover personal resiliency.

FINAL THOUGHTS

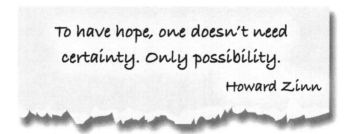

To have hope, one doesn't need certainty. Only possibility.

Howard Zinn

My desire is that this small book does just that: offer hope. With positivity, energy, and purpose, may you open doors to discover more ways to be adaptable, to find ideas and encouragement from others, to respond with agility as you try new actions, and ultimately to continue to create a future that brings you alive with laughter and alignment.

Remember the word *cultivate*. Resiliency requires cultivation. No garden grows with tilling the soil, weeding, watering, and finding what plants grow best in your garden. Effort always precedes reward—even in the dictionary.

Here's to YOUR resilient spirit and your presilient power. May you grow forward!

Eileen McDargh

P.S. To keep you on the road of resiliency; here is a link to a special page on my web site where I will regularly post books, articles, and online resources.

http://www.eileenmcdargh.com/your-resiliency-GPS

Addendum

RESILIENCY ASSESSMENT

What is Your Personal RQ—Resiliency Quotient

Using the following scale put a numerical value by each statement.

Numerical Scale: 1. Never 2. A few times 3. Frequently 4. Without a doubt

1. I believe in my ability to influence my attitude. ___

2. I've handled challenges before, and I can do it again. ___

3. I can look at a problem from many angles. ___

4. I have work that is meaningful. ___

5. I have a strong support network. ___

6. I exercise on a regular basis. ___

7. I clearly communicate my ideas. ___

8. I am appreciated for what I do. ___

9. People say I have a good sense of humor. ___

10. I can see more than one option in a given situation. ___

11. I am generally an optimistic person. ___

12. By my own definition, I believe in a "Higher Power." ___

13. I easily express gratitude. ___

14. I ask for help when I need it. ___

15. I am willing to try new things, to risk. ___

Score:

52-60: What a Rock! You're on a hero's journey!

42-51: Good resilience intentions. See what areas might need improvement?

32-41: Time to get some help. In what areas can you get the fastest, most visible results? Build from there. You might consider hiring a coach.

15-31: Remember the dinosaurs? They did *not* grow forward. And they did NOT GROW through.

Look at the low-scoring responses for growth opportunities. Go back through the book and see what strategies you can find.

RESILIENCY ASSESSMENT

What is Your Organizational RQ—Resiliency Quotient

Using the following scale, put a numerical value by each statement.

Numerical Scale: 1. Never 2. A few times 3. Frequently 4. Without a doubt

1. Employees readily talk about how much they like working here. ___

2. Management is known for asking employees their opinions. ___

3. Management is known for listening to employees' opinions. ___

4. Training is available for all employees on a regular basis. ___

5. Managers are acknowledged for helping employees advance in skill level. ___

6. The organization has flexible work hours. ___

7. People are treated as "whole people" with lives outside work. ___

8. Management is willing to try new things. ___

9. Management readily shares current information about the health of the company.

    ___

10. Managers have superb communication skills.

    ___

11. The organization walks its talk. ___

12. Managers encourage innovation and creativity.

    ___

13. We trust senior management to act in the best interest of all stakeholders. ___

14. We are told bad news as well as good news.

    ___

15. Our company's product/service is meaningful and valuable in the marketplace. ___

16. We are known for carefully listening to the marketplace, the customers, trends, and the competition. ___

Score:

52-64: What a Rock! It's an organization of heroes!

42-52: Good resiliency intentions. See what areas might need improvement. What can YOU do?

32-41: The organization needs help. Who needs to be involved? In what areas can you get the fastest, most visible results? Is this a training issue? Where is your sphere of influence? Build from there. You might need some outside help.

31- 15: Remember the dinosaurs? Grow forward they did NOT. Nor did they GROW through! Time to get serious. Are there too many changes? Does the culture need to have a serious adjustment? What is in your sphere of influence?

Look at the low scoring responses for growth opportunities. Do you see a theme? Go back through the book and see what strategies you can find.

If all else fails call me 949-496-8640.

Optional
Exercises

THE COST OF CHEER

Write down five things that make you happy—
whether walking the in the woods, calling an old
friend, whatever. Take the first five that come to
your mind.

Next to each item, estimate the cost. Estimate how
much time it takes. What do you discover? What's
stopping you?

INNER RESILIENCE: YOUR
PAST IS A PROLOGUE

Jot down three of the most devastating experiences
you have had. Next to them, list the corresponding
insights or lessons you gained as a result. What does
this tell you? What strengths did you use? Do you still
have those strengths?

ACCENTUATE THE POSITIVE

Notice your surroundings. What might be good about the current situation? What are three positive things? According to Dr. Barbara Fredrickson, it takes three positives to overcome a negative and can actually serve as a catalyst to bring more of what you WANT into your life.

FROM SCARCITY TO ABUNDANCE

List ten things you thought there wouldn't be enough of and you survived. List ten areas where you have too much, not too little. List 20-1000 wonderful things that entered your life right at the right time with no effort on your part. Start with air, sun, rain, and more.

A single grateful thought raised to heaven is the most perfect prayer.
Gotthold Ephraim Lessing

KEEP A GRATITUDE LOGBOOK

This is one of the most powerful tools. I've done it on and off for years. Life is much better when I write! Get a blank book, different from the presilience logbook. Every night, write at least three things you are grateful for. Some days, it might be as simple as air and clean sheets. Don't stop. There's more!

DEVELOP A WANT LIST AND A HAVE-TO-DO LIST

Are you living the life you REALLY want? So often, we make changes because we feel we HAVE to do it or we consume irreplaceable time doing "have to do" things. Make a list of ALL the things you have to do. Then, go back and honestly ask if the heavens will fall and your life implode if you crossed some off?

Now, create a list of things you really want to do. Put down everything, even those as crazy as swim with alligators (ugh—maybe you are doing that now), take a world cruise, whatever. Think wide. Think deep. Put a star by those things that are really deeply-felt desires. What steps can you take to move toward them? Remember, small steps matter. Celebrate small wins. Find out who can help you. And grow through this opportunity!

Pick-You-Up
Quotes

TO BOOST UP, BUILD UP,
AND BREAK OUT
YOUR RESILIENT SPIRIT

Keep your spirits up, don't allow yourself to be depressed, and never for one moment doubt but that matters will finish better and more quickly than you imagine.
Napoleon Bonaparte

The secret of change is to focus all your energy not on fighting the old, but on building the new.
Socrates

You can't prevent birds of sorrow flying over your head, but you can prevent them from building nests in your hair.
Chinese proverb

It's better to be a 3-legged coyote than a 4-legged fur coat.
Joe Tye

Fear does not prevent death. It prevents living.
Naguib Mahfouz

*To live is to suffer. To survive is to find
meaning in the suffering.*
Viktor Frankl

*Being defeated is often a temporary condition. Giving up
is what makes it permanent.*
Marilyn vos Savant, American columnist

*Now that my house has fallen down,
I have a better view of the world.*
Zen Buddhist

Failure is the opportunity to begin again more intelligently.
Henry Ford

When your dreams turn to dust, it's time to vacuum.
Anonymous

*The majority of the tragedies that have occurred in my life
have happened only in my mind.*
Michel Eyquem de Montaigne (1533-92 AD)

*God grant me the serenity to accept the things I cannot
change, the courage to change the things I can and the
wisdom to know the difference.*
Reinhold Niebuhr

*Everything will be all right in the end. So if it's not
all right, it's not yet the end.*
Best Exotic Marigold Hotel

In the midst of winter, I found there was, within me, an
invincible summer. And that makes me happy.
For it says that no matter how hard the world pushes against
me, within me, there's something stronger – something
better, pushing right back.
Camus, The Stranger

You never know how STRONG you are
until STRONG is the only choice you have.
Bob Marley

The difference between stupidity and genius is
that genius has its limits.
Albert Einstein

Trying to be happy by accumulating possessions is like trying
to satisfy hunger by taping sandwiches all over your body.
George Carlin

If it is important to you, you'll find a way.
If it is not, you'll find an excuse.
Anon

Only the heart that hurts has the right to joy.
Lewis Smedes

Brick walls are not there to stop you. They are there to make
you prove how much you want something.
Randy Pausch, The Last Lecture

There is no better time to dream new and bigger dreams than when your world has been turned upside down. There's also no more important time for you to stop doing the things that have not been working for you and to start doing things you've never done before.
Joe Tye

When you arise in the morning, give thanks for the morning light, for your life and strength. Give thanks for your food, and the joy of living. If you see no reason for giving thanks, the fault lies with yourself.
Tecumseh, Shawnee Chief

Plenty of people miss their share of happiness, not because they never found it, but because they didn't stop to enjoy it.
William Feather

If you're not enjoying the journey the destination will be a disappointment.
McZen

All who wander are not lost.
Tolkien, Lord of the Rings

Every time we prevail – if even for a moment – over anxiety, fear of failure, feelings of vulnerability and inferiority, we are not left even. We are not as we were; we are ahead. With each obstacle we conquer, we grow larger.
Walter Anderson, The Confidence Course

Recommended Reading

INNER RESILIENCE:

» *Happiness: Unlocking the Mysteries of Psychological Wealth* by Ed Diener, Ph.D.

» *The Art of Resilience: 100 Paths To Wisdom And Strength in An Uncertain World* by Carol Orsborn

» *The How of Happiness: A New Approach to Getting the life You Want* by Sonja Lyubomirsky

» *The Happiness Advantage* by Shawn Achor

RESILIENCE RESEARCH:

» *Resilience: The Science of Mastering Life's Greatest Challenges* by Steven Southwick and Dennis Charney

» *Resilience: Why Things Bounce Back* by Andrew Zolli. (Note: his work looks at such things as biological systems, coral reefs, power grids, communities, and global events where we are losing ground and need to recapture that which is lost. In this case, his term of "bounce" back is appropriate. However, he also has keen insights on how to GROW though the challenge and create a stronger response. Not an easy read but an important one!)

OPTIMISM:

» *Learned Optimism: How to Change Your Mind and Your Life* by Martin Seligman

» *Positivity* by Barbara Fredrickson, Ph.D.

ORGANIZATIONAL RESILIENCE:

» *All Hands on Deck: 8 Essential Lessons for Building a Culture of Ownership* by Joe Tye

» *Leadership and the Art of the Struggle: How Great leaders Grow through Challenge and Adversity* by Steven Snyder

» *The Florence Prescription* (for healthcare) by Joe Tye

» *The Happiness Advantage* by Shawn Achor

» *Leaders Open Doors* by Bill Treasurer

» *What's Your Golden Goldfish: The Vital Few: All Customers and Employees Are Not Created Equal* by Stan Phelps

» *The Discomfort Zone: How Leaders Turn Difficult Conversations into Breakthroughs* by Marcia Reynolds

PERSONAL RESILIENCE:

» *The Resiliency Advantage* by Al Siebert

» *The Way of Transition* by William Bridges

» *AdaptAbility: How to Survive Change You Didn't Ask For* by M.J. Ryan

» *Happiness: Unlocking the Mysteries of Psychological Wealth* by Ed Diener, Ph.D.

» *The Art of Resilience: 100 Paths To Wisdom And Strength in An Uncertain World* by Carol Orsborn

» *The How of Happiness: A New Approach to Getting the life You Want* by Sonja Lyubomirsky

» *Accidental Genius: Using Writing to Generate Your Best Ideas, Insight, and Content* by Mark Levy

» *The Happiness Advantage* by Shawn Achor

» *Shed or You're Dead!* by Kathy Dempsey

» *Personal Resilience for Up, Down or Sideways: How to Succeed When Time are Good, Bad or In-between* by Mark Sanborn

SUPPORT NETWORK:

» *Mutuality Matters* by Kare Anderson

» *True North Groups* by Bill George and Doug Baker

AGILITY:

» *Play: How It Shapes the Brain, Opens the Imagination, and Invigorates the Soul* by Stuart Brown and Christopher Vaughan

» *ConZENtrate: Get Focused and Pay Attention - When Life is Filled with Pressures, Distractions, and Multiple Priorities* by Sam Horn

» *Do More Great Work* by Michael Bungay Stanier

ALIGNMENT:

» *Finding Your Way in a Wild New World* by Martha Beck

» *Love It! Don't Leave It* by Beverly Kaye and Sharon Jordan-Evans

» *A Hidden Wholeness* by Parker Palmer

» *Body of Work: Finding the Thread That Ties Your Story Together* by Pamela Slim

» *Full Steam Ahead-Unleash the Power of Vision in Your Work and Your Life by* Ken Blanchard and Jesse Lyn Stoner

» *The Highest Goal: The Secret That Sustains You in Every Moment* by Michael Ray

About the Author

EILEEN MCDARGH, CEO- CHIEF ENERGY OFFICER

Since founding her consulting firm in 1980, Eileen McDargh has helped organizations and individuals transform the life of their business and the business of their life through conversations that matter and connections that count. She believes that resiliency is a critical life skill and one that requires the energy of connections.

She draws upon practical business know-how, life's experiences and years of consulting to major national and international organizations that have ranged from global pharmaceuticals to the US Armed Forces, from health care associations to religious institutions. Her programs are content rich, interactive, provocative and playful—even downright hilarious.

Executive Excellence magazine continually ranked her as one of **the top 50 thought leaders in self-leadership development. Global Gurus International**, a British-based provider of resources for leadership, communication and sales training, also **named her in 2013 as one of the World's Top 30 Leadership Professionals following a global survey of 22,000 business professionals.**

She Authored

» *Work for a Living & Still Be Free to Live*

» *The Resilient Spirit: Heart Talk for Surviving In An Upside Down World*

» *Talk Ain't Cheap—It's Priceless*

» *Gifts from the Mountain: Simple Truths for Life's Complexities*

» *My Get Up and Go Got Up & Went*

As a business author and commentator, Eileen has appeared on network news, on radio programs and in business journals and in major metropolitan newspapers.

Eileen is a certified speaking professional (CSP) and her election into the CPAE Speaker Hall of Fame places her among the top 3% of speakers in the United States.

She's also listed as a recommended expert through the Sloan Work and Family Research Network now headquartered at University of Penna.

You can reach Eileen at:

» Twitter: @macdarling

» LinkedIn: https://www.linkedin.com/in/eileenmcdargh

» Facebook: http://www.facebook.com/speakereileen

» Website: http://www.eileenmcdargh.com

» Email: Eileen@eileenmcdargh.com

Resources for this book along with more recommended readings and programs will be updated online. You can check it out here:

http://www.eileenmcdargh.com/Your-Resiliency-GPS